WITCHES
Coloring Book
VINTY
PRINTS

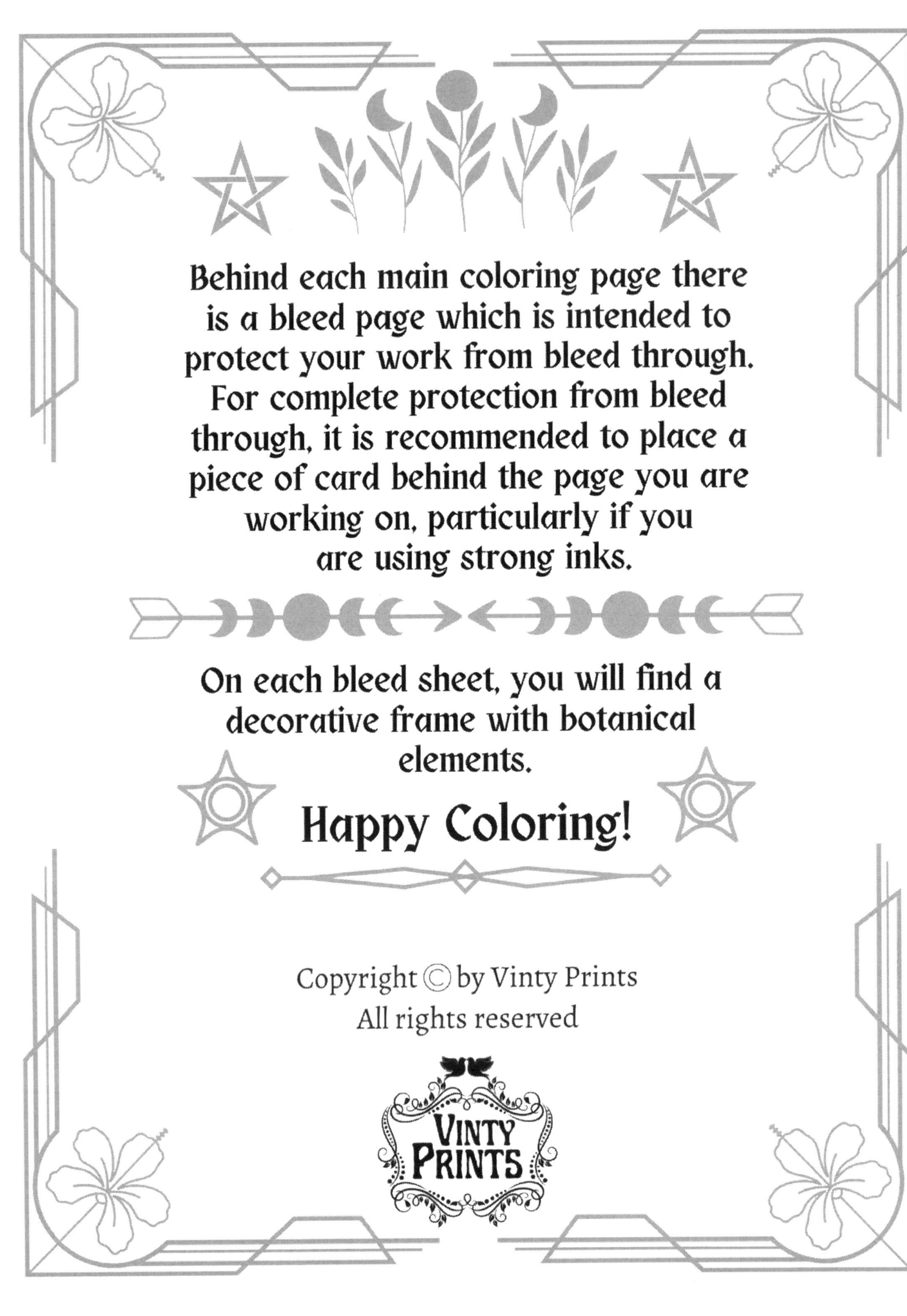

Behind each main coloring page there is a bleed page which is intended to protect your work from bleed through. For complete protection from bleed through, it is recommended to place a piece of card behind the page you are working on, particularly if you are using strong inks.

On each bleed sheet, you will find a decorative frame with botanical elements.

Happy Coloring!

Blessed
are the
Witches

Be the
Witch
you were
born to be,
magic, happy,
wild and free!

There is a little
witch
in all of us!

One with the night,
one with the day,
one with the Earth,
that is the witches way

WITCHCRAFT
is a deep love of
nature and the
ability to see magic
in places where
others do not.

THE UNIVERSE REVEALS
IT'S SECRETS TO THOSE
WHO DARE TO FOLLOW
THEIR HEARTS.

You say
Witch
like it's a bad
thing!

YOU DON'T NEED MAGIC
TO BELIEVE IN MAGIC
YOU ARE MAGIC
YOU NEED TO
BELIEVE IN
YOURSELF!

Always Trust
Your Inner
Goddess

REAL MAGIC IS NOT
ABOUT GAINING POWER
OVER OTHERS, IT'S
ABOUT GAINING POWER
OVER YOURSELF.

IN MAGIC
YOU ARE THE
MAIN INGREDIENT

Under Your
SPELL

THE POWER OF
NATURE

Always be yourself.
Unless you can
be a
Witch
then always
be a witch!

Made in the USA
Middletown, DE
02 December 2022